<u>Introduction</u>

In order to get yourself prepared to succeed financially you have to make sure you have the right mindset. It is most important that you convince yourself you can achieve your objectives. Mainstream schools still teach the same outdated lessons of generations ago, which is "do well in school get a good education and find good secure job." While that advice may have been good forty years ago, in this day and age of financial austerity and globalization many business have closed down or off-shored and even many service company's are seeking to maximise their profits by sending even skilled jobs off shore.

Who hasn't received a call from their friendly local service company only to find the caller is from the other side of the world?

In many parts of the world the era of secure job with good pay and conditions is quickly coming to an end which is why it is more important now more then ever that people start seeking financial security rather job security.

This can be difficult for many people as from a young age society has instilled what I call the "middle-class mindset" in most people which can prevent them from succeeding in another sphere other then employment even if they hate their job or gainful employment is limited.

Without the right mindset and priorities financial freedom is not possible.

How many people feel lost when they lose their job? How many after they lose their job will lose everything else because they cannot find another job to pay their debts or bills?

Other people dream of financial freedom, buy books about strategies which create wealth, read the first fifty pages and jump into the first investment or get rich quick scheme that comes their way. As you'd expect that person will probably fail. Maybe the strategies were good but his poor mindset ruined his chance of success.

The wealthy have a totally different mindset to the middle-class and therefore short of winning the lottery, a person seeking financial freedom cannot succeed with the mindset or skill set taught to us in school.

The aim of this book is to help equip people seeking financial success with the same basic mindset that wealthy people have.

It is my hope that after reading this book you will come away with a new outlook on the path you wish to pursue to your financial success.

<u>Contents</u>

Chapter 1

Chapter 2

Chapter 3

Chapter 4

Chapter 5

Chapter 6

Chapter 7

Chapter 8

Chapter 9

Chapter 1

How We Think

This chapter will give you tips on how to think about cash the way the wealthy do. It will help you become financially smarter also.

Assets Or Obligations?

The greatest misconception about being wealthy is that you have to flaunt your wealth to show individuals that you're wealthy. Believe it or not, there might be millionaire families on your street and you'd never know it.

That's because most millionaires look like regular individuals who don't flaunt their wealth. They own regular houses and auto-mobiles. They might have a few luxuries but most average millionaires can't be spotted on a daily basis as they prefer it to be that way and don't show off their wealth.

You have to memorize the difference between an asset and a financial obligation. An asset is something that puts cash in your pocket without you having to execute much work for it.

A financial obligation is something that takes cash out of your pockets and doesn't put cash in your pocket. If you wish to be wealthy, you demand to acquire as many assets as possible and do away with as many financial obligations as possible.

The wealthy are concerned with educating their youngsters on the importance of having a good financial education as opposed to a common, more traditional education youngsters are taught in school. They know their youngsters aren't going to study financial skills in school on how to produce cash with their ideas and businesses or learn the info they require to get wealthy and stay that way. Consequently, you need to teach your youngster the real rules of cash and value that education a bit more than a college education. I'm not telling you to tell your youngster not to go to school. I'm telling you to instruct them in the importance of having a great financial education.

The wealthy are concerned with producing as much passive revenue as they may and working less and less for earned revenue. This, they know will help them continue getting wealthier and richer. You goal ought to be to earn as much passive revenue as you potentially can and convert earned revenue from a occupation into passive revenue.

Be open-minded. It is so simple to have preconceived notions on a matter, but fight the urge and listen to the statement or issue presented to you. Don't draw to speedy conclusions even if they look apparent. Think of it as attempting to solve a mystery on TV. The evident answer is rarely the correct one. Reaching the answer involves gathering facts and discarding biases.

Believe outside the box. I'm sure you've heard this phrase but it's the critical thinker's motto. Believe differently than everyone else. It's simpler said than done but a trick I utilize isn't reading or listening to others ideas until I have drawn my own conclusions. It's so simple to be drawn into one way of thinking once hearing another's ideas so do your best to abstain till you trust you've solved the issue.
A different trick I find helpful is to try and believe like a youngster. I know this appears silly, but it's amazing how young kids may solve riddles before adults may. They believe on a completely dissimilar level and rarely over-believe things as most adults do. It all calls for practice.
Explore statements. I can't say enough on this matter. Erroneous statements are made daily and "poor" thinkers take them and run.

They don't bother to check the facts for truth; it's much easier not to. They'll eventually look like fools when the garbage they've been repeating is proven false and any believability they had will be gone. Believability is everything.
Check your facts before you repeat them and you'll gain believability and the respect of other people.

Chapter 2

What We Bring About in Our Lives

If you've ever seen 'The Secret' then you're likely convinced that the Law of Attraction is real and it works. But you may be wondering what you're doing wrong since you are able to manifest pocket change, and perhaps a gratis cup of coffee , or perhaps even a 5 dollar bill on the floor of the supermarket, but you're having a hassle stepping it up to anything life changing. Keep reading for a couple of pointers.

What We Get

Keep increasing your awareness. My fresh theory is this: Your power to manifest your wants is directly corresponding to the amount of awareness you have. Attempt to notice when you are saying damaging words, or believing damaging thoughts and repeat them directly in a positive and affirming way.
You are attracting those damaging topics to yourself, rather than great matters that you may still trust you don't deserve or you can't possess. We all merit everything we ever wanted and more. It's an issue of working with our own personalities and energy flows to work out how to draw in those matters.

To evidence cash you must be specific with cash. You must produce and design affirmations about cash and financial abundance. As frequently as you may think of it, say aloud, or to yourself, 'I'm a cash magnet. I merit financial abundance. I'm now drawing in all of my wildest desires. There's more than enough cash for everybody, including me.'

These phrases and sentences will pick your energy vibrations up to an elevated level, and help to re-train your brain to believe and live inside an abundant life-style.

This likewise helps you to be alert to any fresh chances, which come your way. Let's face it. 1000000 dollars is likely not going to turn up in a suitcase on your porch, unless you get into some truly fishy stuff. You are likely going to have to make some sort of moves in order to produce that 1000000 bucks, so you are going to want your brain to be prepared to pick up on the hints.

When you start drawing in abundance in little ways, it will get simpler to appreciate, have gratitude, and draw in matters, which YOU see as larger and more crucial. Don't forget, it's all the same to the world. It's you who trusts you're allowed to draw in a new auto. Cash is cash to the universe, and abundance comes in all forms.

This is a great one. This is the one that's working for me. I've studied and read about the Law of Attraction and I recognize that damaging be-gets more damaging, and favourable vibration brings abundance. What I was lacking was the fretting. I may say a hundred times a day, 'I'm a cash magnet,' but I was still fretting and fussing about paying the bills, mending the car, purchasing food, etc.

Until I realized that, the subconscious fretting wasn't assisting my cause one bit. It's hard to go that deep into your lifelong thought blueprints and release profoundly embedded power blocks, unless you are able to talk to a pro. So rather than attempting to trick myself OUT of fretting about cash, I chose to begin fretting about the opposite.

Today I worry about what the heck I'm going to do with all this cash. Every time I catch myself fretting, I change the target of what I'm fretting about. I've determined that my accountant will be truly upset with me as I bought a Porsche for each day of the week, rather than just the one that we budgeted. I likewise wonder how I'm going to keep all these disbursals straight, as I have so much cash, I truly don't want individuals taking advantage of me.

I grew up pitiful, so I'm not totally certain I know how to handle all this cash. I'm so worried that I may now hire the right individuals to keep track of all these trips, auto mobiles, houses and jets that I now own.

In order to bring about cash, you have to work out your own personal relationship with cash and tweak it. Work out how you feel about cash, if you have any dark and deeply implanted opinions or reactions towards cash, or if you've learned a particular thought pattern regarding cash.
Increase your cognizance, recite cash affirmations, and if you are a worrier, simply begin fretting about what the heck you are going to do with all this cash.

Chapter 3

Planing For Success

The older adage that "nice guys come in last" is likely simply that--an older adage. Many experts state that being prepared is your most beneficial bet for success.

Readiness comes in a lot of different forms. An athlete gears up his body for competition by training, a pupil sets up her brain for an examination by studying and a policeman with intense training. When one's body and brain are correctly prepared, the psychological effect of turning into a winner is greatly heightened.

In order to understand how to get to be a winner, you likewise have to learn how to lose. Valuable lessons may be acquired by losing. It is significant to remember that losing isn't an indictment of your inability; instead, it ought to be viewed as a learning tool utilized to better your skills. The act of losing may be made positive by managing future emotions and analysing pitiful performance.

Many psychologists believe it's hard, if not nearly inconceivable, to win without first founding a distinct set of goals. Your goals, all the same, have to be accomplishable and not beyond fair expectations. Formulating goals, your blueprint for success, is the first step to winning.

Simply as crucial as establishing an honest set of goals is envisioning success. If an individual can't see being a winner, he never will. At large, many individuals find it less nerve-wracking to "not lose" than to win.

Too many individuals, losing is easier than winning. Winning is a composite process that involves preparedness, training, dedication and goals, a formula that frequently is beyond the mental ability of many. Those who have the power to envision themselves as winners get simply that with preparedness and dedication.

If you've never won, winning means redefining yourself. For many, it's merely easier to remain the same individual you've always been instead of get somebody whom other people will hold in elevated regard, envy and even criticize.

In order to get to be a winner, you have to prepare, produce goals, and acquire a vision and act. Plainly put, believing that it is simply as easy to win as to lose and abiding by a design for success will go a long way to accomplishing your winning goal, whether it be in sports, family or career or money.

Chapter 4

Do You Play To Lose Or Win?

Of all the fabled sports figures, golf's Tiger Woods frequently is the first who comes to your brain when you entertain the psychology of winning.
But the mentality of a winner goes far past the sporting fields of competition; instead, it extends to relationships, family, career, and money. Much of winning is a mental stake, a readiness by design, a design preplanned in your brain.

To succeed in any sphere in life you need to have a positive mental outlook and take full responsibility for your actions and your life. If you are one of those people that blame people or other external factors for your lack of success then this could be what is stopping you "making it". Not taking responsibility for your own destiny and blaming others for your lack of success for example "the boss doesn't like me" or "it's who you know not what you know", can be a very damaging way to go through life.

You cannot control the changes that take place in the

world or the economy but YOU can control how you react to these changes and what positive steps you can take to succeed.

Success in any in any sphere of life requires one to have a positive mental attitude and for you to take full responsibility for your life.
 If you are one of those people that blame people or other external factors for your lack of success then this could be what is stopping you "making it". Not taking responsibility for your own destiny and blaming others for your lack of success for example "the coach does not like me" or "they only pick their friends", can be a very damaging way to go through life.
With the above mental outlook people can give up completely, I know, I fallen into this trap myself in the past. However the problem is often not circumstances at all. The problem is often with the person and his or her mindset. People with this type of thinking will not make it in any area of their life unless they change their mindset, this change is very possible if you want it to be. Please read on and maybe this will help you reach your goals or maybe give you that edge you are looking for.
People with a winning mentality in any field are active and always looking for ways to improve

themselves. They see failure and rejection as temporary obstacles that must be overcome, not as career ending events. When confronted by a problem, people with a winning mentality immediately start to look for ways of overcoming the problem. People with a losing mentality will usually stop in their tracks and look for something or someone they can blame, they will usually try to find excuses to justify their attitude, it's always someone else's fault and never their own.

The reality is you can achieve anything you want in life if you want it badly enough and look for and implement ways to achieve it.

It only takes a slight change in the way you think. By seeing problems or as challenges that must be overcome will give you the impetus to try harder and work harder to overcome these minor setbacks.

When everything seems to be going against me I remind my self of a quote be Henry Ford *"When everything seems to be going against you, remember an airplane takes off against the wind, not with it."*

Chapter 5

Don't Dream It, Do It!

You are able to achieve any goal if you work at it, trust in yourself and treat every setback as an opportunity to learn and improve. Regardless what you wish to accomplish, whether it's singing with a rock group, beginning your own business or becoming wealthy, abide by these steps and you will soon be well on your way to the life you've always conceived of.

Are You A Dreamer Or A Doer?

The first reason most individuals don't get what they wish is that they don't know what they wish. Wealthy individuals are totally clear that they want wealth. They're unwavering in their desire. They are totally dedicated to creating wealth. As long as it's legal, ethical, and moral, they'll do whatever it takes to have wealth. Rich individuals don't send mixed messages to the universe. Poor individuals do. Remain positive. Acquaintances, neighbours and colleagues might tell you why you can't accomplish your goal. Simply disregard them and carry on pursuing your dream till you achieve it. Cast out thoughts of failure from your psyche as soon as they come up. There's scientific evidence that favourable thought does work, so turn over that fact if you have temporary doubts about accomplishing your goal.

Figure out a plan. Decide on a goal and then work out what you have to do to get there. It might call for taking classes, slimming down, moving to a different city or something as challenging as producing a movie. Arrange small goals, like stepping stones, to your ultimate accomplishment. Reward yourself each time you accomplish one of these mini-goals.

Write it down. Sustain a success journal or diary. Arrive at lists of what you need to achieve each day to accomplish your goal. Draw pictures or cut out magazine clippings to prompt you and remind you of your wanted results.

Envision the desired result. Think about being a successful, confident business owner or wealthy or whatsoever you wish to be. Keep your goal perpetually on the "front burner" till you achieve it.

Hang in. Some days the road to your goal will run more swimmingly than others, but never misplace faith. Step back and alter your approach if the situation merits it. Remember the saying "Rome wasn't built in a day" and don't quit, even if things appear bleak.

Learn from other people. Talk to others who have accomplished the same goal you're going after. If you wish to be wealthy, contact other wealthy people or frequent message boards associated to that. By finding out how others achieved the same goal, you'll learn what to do and what to keep away from.

Read inspirational books and sayings. From "The Seven Spiritual Laws of Success" by Deepak Chopra to old favourites like "Think and Grow Rich" by Napoleon Hill, select from a plethora of books to keep you motivated and give you new thoughts.

Chapter 6

Are You Thinking Big?

Our culture cannot seem to make up its mind about the value of ambition. On the one hand, we praise those who work hard and accomplish hard goals. On the other hand, we put individuals down for being selfish and power-hungry, and we frequently take pleasure in seeing powerful celebrities fall.

No wonder so many individuals have assorted feelings about being ambitious. On top of that, the goals they wished they cared more about might not truly be their own. In order to settle conflicts about ambition, you have to get a clearer thought of what you truly wish.

How To Expand The Scope Of Your Thinking

Enquire of yourself what you think you ought to be accomplishing. Then enquire of yourself if that is something you truly wish to accomplish, or if you are attempting to live out somebody else's notion of what you ought to be doing. Sometimes a lack of ambition is a sign that you are protesting doing something that is not correct for you.

Think about what you'd accomplish if you could accomplish anything and didn't have to worry about cash. Write out your purpose in life in one sentence. Try out career counselling or self-help books if you are not certain what you wish to accomplish. Lack of ambition might stem from not having discovered goals that are correct for you.

Enquire of yourself if you are so frightened of failing that you would rather not even attempt to accomplish your goals. Fear of failure may be a dream killer. Becoming cognizant of your fear is the first step in addressing it.

Break down your goals into littler, more manageable chunks if you are experiencing overwhelming feelings. Take one step at a time, and give yourself pay-offs for your progress. If you have given up and lost ambition because your goals looked out of the question, you might simply have to organize your work differently.

Ways to help yourself think big include:

- **Getting into the Right Frame of Mind.** Life in general is a marathon not a sprint. It's easy to succumb to the feeling of urgency to do everything now. But fatigue can mean sabotage for you as well as your personal life. Prioritize longevity and keep one eye on your ultimate objective. Think about what pace you need to set now to maintain your stamina and enthusiasm for years to come.

- **Break every job into smaller jobs.** Any time you are overwhelmed by the enormity of what your try to do just list out what you need to do to achieve your final objective and break it down into smaller jobs and focus on finishing one job at a time. Remember even the pyramids in Egypt were built one stone at a time.

- **Establishing good habits** and resisting bad ones can go a long way to preventing fatigue. Find strategies for staying on track and sticking to achieving your objectives.

- **Experiment**. What changes are you going to make to your life How will you know when you've succeeded? While these questions help you focus on your mission they don't exactly inspire a neat step-by-process. And the truth is that there may be many other method instead of one clear "right" answer. Instead of going with a pre-determined and hypothetical outcome, find clarity by trying more then one strategy.

- **Read history.** The history books are full of people who started small and went on to achieve great things. Find someone who has succeed in the area in which you aim to succeed in and study their life. Do some research to find how they began. Learn from their success and failures and take note of their turning points and milestones. By learning how they got to where they ended up helps demystify your objectives and helps you understand that greatest people in history are only humans like yourself and that like yourself they all started from somewhere. It's also helpful to learn that all successful people had doubts and doubters of their own.

- Forget the idea of overnight success, when somebody finally "makes it" most people only see the successful person, they don't see the hard work and the many setbacks that person endured before they became successful.

- Keep your focus on building your long term momentum, establish good habits and take small steps to help build momentum that will take you closer to your goals.

- Give yourself permission to be ambitious. Ambition might have a bad reputation some of the times, however if you act ethically and set worthy goals, there is nothing wrong with working hard to accomplish them and nothing wrong with wishing to acquire credit for what you have done.

- Ask yourself if you wish to live a hard-driving competitory life or if you prefer to be easygoing or something in-between. The more you get in touch with what you truly wish, the happier you are in all likelihood to be.

Chapter 7

Turn Problems into Opportunity s.

Once you dwell on the damaging aspects of life and equate your failings to another's successes, you are able to become depressed and discouraged. You have heard that a positive mental attitude will better your outlook; however, you might find it hard to see the silver lining once dark clouds loom.

Every problem carries it's equivalent size of opportunity, however, most people focus on the problems itself instead of the solutions or opportunities these problems can provide.

When we focus on the problems rather then the solution we are focusing our energy negatively. However success can only be achieved when we turn problems into opportunities.

At times this can be difficult, but in order to positively archive your objectives, you need to focus on finding solutions. Think of the problems in your life and start looking for ways you can achieve your goals. The answer may not come easily the first time.

Once you understand that opportunities are all around you that's when you can really change your life. When you open yourself up to looking for solutions to your problems that's when you will begin to attract opportunities to you.

This is all part of using your mind to change how you see your problems. When you see everything as an opportunity, instead of a problem your focus will begin to shift. Before you know it, you will begin to experience real, lasting changes that will have a powerful effect on your life and future success.

One day Thomas Edison, seeing the problems associated with using candles and oil lanterns for illumination decided that maybe electricity could be used to provide light so he took up where Humphry Davy (the person to created the first light globe) left off and created a light which operated on electricity. He tried and failed ten thousand times before he created the first, reliable and marketable light globe, but I think you will agree that his invention changed the world as we know it.

Some of the most successful people in history achieved their success by finding solutions to problems other people just lived with or ignored.

Chapter 8

Taking A Good, Hard Look at yourself

Live for yourself. Once you perpetually attempt to be the person other people wish you to be, you cheat yourself out of individuality and your own aspirations. Take a long hard look at what you wish out of life and design your daily routine to include at least one or two elements that cause you to get your goals closer.

Comprehend that even if you can't control outside conditions, you are able to controller your response to them. If you are currently working in a dead-end job with a boss who's degrading, make a conscious effort to tell yourself that his poor behaviour may make you upset only if you let it.

Leave your work at the office, mentally that is. Once you step outside after a stressful day's work, tell yourself that you have all day tomorrow to deal with the troubles and mentally switch gears by thinking something favourable or planning your future vacation, even if it's months away.

Slow up. Once constantly pressed to finish tasks, you are able to develop a damaging mental attitude towards life. If time is a commodity, work out how you are able to schedule your chores more efficiently.

Simply by getting up 15 minutes earlier every day, you will have the time to say hello to your neighbour, pet a pup or simply gaze out the window at the rain. Learn something new day-after-day. You are able to encourage a positive mental attitude by always providing something fresh in your life. As a youngster, your curiosity led you to explore and learn. Recapture that feeling now by taking a night class, studying a fresh language, learning to garden or anything else that interests you.

Arrive at a list of the favourable aspects in your life. Include your accomplishments. If you are a humorous individual, put that on the list. If you are able to play the violin or you know a lot about dogs, include those aspects. Arrive at a long detailed list of everything that you do well or at least that is not damaging. Read the list once you require a mental boost.

Help other people. Poking out a helping hand to those in need makes you feel needed and worthwhile. Make it a habit to volunteer for charitable organizations. Assisting other people allows us to be grateful for the blessing we have and helps us maintain a favourable mental attitude.

Envision drawing in and receiving cash and wealth. For instance, you may spend several minutes every day seeing yourself receiving checks and money orders in the mail for products or services you sell. You may also cut out photos and images of dollar bills and coins, paste them onto a piece of paper or cardboard and hang the images on your bedroom wall or above your office space at home, places where you frequently go so you see the photos and images many times a day.

Hold favourable feelings or vibrations about cash. By sustaining positive vibrations, you may attract and manifest wealth and cash. "The Law of Attraction" states that like draws in like.

Consequently, if you feel favourable emotions when you consider getting cash, you may draw in more cash into your life. When you see others with cash, feel appreciation for what they have. Each time you get cash, feel great about it and those occurrences will step-up.

Write positive affirmations about wealth and cash. For instance, you may write, "I'm receiving more and more cash each day from the sale of my fresh books and audiotapes." You may likewise speak favourable affirmations.

Composed or spoken, positive affirmations help train your subconscious to produce and find ideas, insights and action steps you may take to get cash. As you continue to write and/or speak favourable affirmations, your subconscious will go on to work to attract the wealth you wish.

Chapter 9

You Are Who Your Friends Are

The saying goes "You are what you eat" then the same is real with what you think and who you hang around with. Having a successful mindset will have to deal with your own thought formulas, thinking, cash habits and who your friends are.

You are who you hang around with - If you acquaintances are all on social welfare then your power to have a millionaire mentality will be limited to a social welfare mentality.

Sadly, we'll need to cut ourselves off from people who are negative thinkers. We'll have to find and make fresh friends who have already succeeded and have the millionaire mindset.

Produce a budget and attend positive motivational seminars. This is likewise a good way to find like-minded people. Also, regardless how boring it may get continue to listen to success audio tapes and CD's or on your MP3 player.

Quit listening to negative journalism. Catch yourself in what you say, do and believe! Are they actions of a millionaire mentality? If not then quit and replace with a more favourable thought and action.

Fake it till you make it! The only way to accomplish a successful mentality is to tell yourself daily morning noon and night that you're successful; you've accomplished success and will accomplish success.

The subconscious mind doesn't know the difference. Soon your thoughts will afford fresh possibilities. Be creative.

Everybody has to begin somewhere and it has utterly nothing to do with race, age, location, parents, training, religion, winning the lottery, being born with a gold spoon in mouth etcetera.

Have fun with the procedure and refuse to let other people (even successful people) to tell you what to think! Utilize your own God given intuition and be great. At the same time, we have to be open-minded and accept to our own errors and learn from them.

Final Words.

The opening move is making a point you have a wealth of support in whatever enterprises you are hoping to accomplish in life. I've always had good mentors in my life that gave me the support I needed when I felt lost or lonely.

It's this support system that keeps you on track; much like a lighthouse keeps transports from crashing into the shore. Consider what produces great value for you in life and go for it. Value is a different word for wealth, and if you're not already aware, individuals are just as gravitated toward wealth as they are value. Learn to honour the riches you already have in your life. It doesn't matter how much you have in your bank account or if your living in a alley. You have to first construct a baseline of what you're grateful for and centre on that as a building block to the following advancement.

What I mean is that you have to be wealthy subjectively before it may manifest objectively.

I'll present you an illustration. You may make 500 dollars an hour and that would sound rich to the average individual, but if you spend 800 dollars an hour on things you believe you want but don't truly need, you'll always be poor regardless how much you bring in.

Produce synergy with all your systems of wealth to acquire more wealth. I'll give you an illustration. I exercise to keep my physical health rich, which in turn makes my mental wealth rich. The gain in mental and physical wealth causes me to acquire more in life, and when I mean more, that could be cash, relationships, power or what have you. Wealth is more about a sort of mentality then it is a physical value, constantly remember that.

www.ingramcontent.com/pod-product-compliance
Lightning Source LLC
Chambersburg PA
CBHW070729180526
45167CB00004B/1680